WHY MUST I MARRY THIS BRUVVA?

THE
CORNERSTONE
PUBLISHING

SEYI HOPEWELL

Unless otherwise noted, all Scripture quotations are from the New King James Version of the Bible. Copyright ©1993, 1996 by Thomas Nelson, Inc. Used by permission. All rights reserved.

WHY MUST I MARRY THIS BRUVVA?
Copyright © 2017 by **Seyi Hopewell**

ISBN: 978-1-944652-38-8

Cornerstone Publishing
A Division Cornerstone Creativity Group LLC
Phone: +1(516) 547-4999
info@thecornerstonepublishers.com
www.thecornerstonepublishers.com

To order this book or for speaking engagement:
Seyi Hopewell
www.seyihopewell.org
+1 832.909.9787
Email: bookthismc@gmail.com

This publication may not be reproduced, stored in a retrieval system, or transmitted in whole or in part, in any form or by any means, electronic, mechanical, photocopying, recording, or otherwise, without the prior written permission of the publisher.
All rights reserved.

Printed in the United States of America

CONTENTS

Dedication...7
Introduction...9

1. Decision Time...13

2. What is Bruvva?...27

3. A Brother—His Attributes...........................47

4. Wisdom is The Key.....................................65

5. Marriage is A Gift..75

6. Put That "Book" Back.................................83

7. This Time...91

About The Author...99

DEDICATION

To Timi and Enny.
You are my gifts from God.
I love you and pray that you will accomplish
MORE!

To my late Father, Elder Olusola Popoola
who went to be with the Lord on July
4th 2007. He spent his life grooming his
children; always believing in their potential
for greatness. I love you always and thank you
for the foundation you laid for me in order
to achieve greatness; continue to rest in peace
Daddy.

INTRODUCTION

How many times have you found yourself in a situation where a crucial decision had to be made but you were at your wits' end, unable to decide what to do or where to go? For most of us, this happens frequently, even at a restaurant where the menu shows a plethora of options to choose from but we cannot decide what to eat for dinner.

Choosing a life partner is definitely not one to be rushed. You need all the time, patience and wisdom that it takes. Choosing a life partner is a decision that should be God-inspired. Hence it is not a decision that should be taken as one would do to a menu option – making a selection based on who fits your desires and the *appetite* you currently have.

Deciding for a mate in such a careless manner has been and continues to be the bane of many marriages. Many of us have fallen into the same error in the past, and this is why this book has been written with lots of practical insights and spiritual principles to keep you from stumbling and safely guide you to a happy and fruitful marital life.

The error most women make first and foremost is in choosing someone that is not compatible with them. There is someone special for every single one of us but we must take our time to choose wisely and let God guide us.

This book describes a 'bruvva' and the bad character traits he possesses yet many women fall victim and continue the relationship for many different reasons. A brother on the other hand has better qualities but due to lack of insight and foresight, many women have missed opportunities to be married to such men; they pass him up because he does not conform to the ideal "picture" they drew as young girls or they measure him up by a false yardstick. It is also important to state that some women choose well and are actually married to 'brothers' yet they demean, disrespect and disregard the power, plan and purpose of such good men.

As you read, you will find nuggets to get you inspired, revelations to get you emancipated, illustrations to get you enlightened, assurances to keep you encouraged, as well as exhortations to get you empowered to achieve your marital dreams and fulfill your true destiny.

Seyi Hopewell
2017

CHAPTER 1
DECISION TIME

It was decision time for Mina. The house was quiet – except for the ticking of the clock and the pounding of her heart. Steve had popped the question and she had promised to think it through and give him an answer in a week's time. And here she was in her room, six days later, still so confused and panicky. She had bitten off every nail on her fingers and tapped on her computer table till there was no more rhythm in her tap. Frustrated with the prolonged conflict between her head and her heart, she blurted out: "I need to make a decision!"

That was a 24-year-old outspoken, bubbly lady, in the prime of her life, full of character and class. A bachelor's degree holder and friend to many, she had spent much of her time counseling others and lending a helping hand to the needy. Now, she needed help. She was stuck with the decision of whether to accept an informal proposal from the man in her life.

Before I proceed, let me drop the first of several nuggets you will receive throughout the course of reading this book. The nuggets are inspired thoughts to help singles realize the root causes of marital crisis and divorce, in the hope that they will avoid the same mistakes that many have made. Eat the nuggets my friend; they will keep you full and you will thank me later.

Nugget 1
Marry the man you are most compatible with and not the man in your life or the one who proposes first, and you will be safe.

Yes, there is a big difference!

Now, back to Mina, here are some important questions to consider:

1. Why was she stuck, since Steve was the only man in her life?
2. Why was she panicky?
3. Why did she feel pressured to make a decision?
4. Why was she not elated at the news of a proposal?
5. Why was she so confused?
6. Why did she need a week to give him an answer?

You will be able to answer these questions easily when you are done reading this book. But, for now, let me just say that seven years after that day of panic and indecision for Mina, she had changed from the 24-year old "social butterfly"—the energetic one who brought flavor to every gathering, the one who frequently organized events and brought friends together, the one who enjoyed public speaking, dancing, travelling and exploring new things with others—to a gloomy, tired, bitter, fearful, hurt and scarred single mother.

Ouch!

What happened? She accepted Steve's proposal and they were married.

Let me land. Please.

Do You Want to Be Complete or Finished?

I read somewhere that the words "complete" and "finished" are often used interchangeably yet they mean different things. The World Dictionary defines complete as either an adjective that means "having all parts or elements, lacking nothing; whole; entire; full—like a complete set of Mark Twain's writings"; or a verb that means "to make whole or entire; as in, I need three more words to complete the puzzle."

In contrast, one of the ways the same dictionary describes finished is "without further hope of success or continuation; as in, she was finished as a prima ballerina."

For Mina, marriage was the next phase of her life. She had completed her bachelor's degree. So, according to her and her family, marriage was next. It soon became a common topic of discussion at every family gathering. Indeed, at every opportunity her father got to speak about his daughter's educational accomplishment, he always concluded with the fact that she was getting married soon.

Nugget 2
Don't allow pressure from parents and other "well-wishers" to derail your future.

Parents are often advised not to pressure their children into marriage, even if they seem "overdue for marriage", as some parents would say. The reason is simple. The pressure placed upon young adults who are not quite ready for marriage is one of the many reasons marriages fail and collapse.

As a lady, the questions you should be asking yourself are: *Does marriage have to be the next phase of my life after completing my G.E.D, bachelor's degree or even a master's degree? Does it have to be the next thing following an accidental pregnancy? Must another marriage be the next step in my life right after a divorce? Or, in fact, is there really a 'right time' to marry?*

My answer to each of the above questions is: no, I do not think so.

Defining Your Status
Where are you at this very moment in your life? If you are married, are you enjoying your marriage or are you simply enduring it and desperately seeking a way to sort things out?

If you are single, where are you in your singleness? Are you going to school? Working full time? Involved in ministry? Raising a child or children alone? Engaged? Divorced? Widowed? Separated? Happy single, living an amazing life, and eyeing the possibility of remarrying? Hurt, and undergoing the healing process? Never been married?

You must fall in one of these categories. Whichever one you fall into, there are certain things you must understand about marriage in order to help yourself and others. Let's consider them.

1. Why God Instituted Marriage
God's intention in Genesis when he made the woman out of the man was to make the man complete. He says in Genesis 2:18, "It is not good that man should be alone; I will make him a helper comparable to him." When God made Eve, Adam looked at her and said "This is now bone of my bone and flesh of my flesh, she shall be called woman, because she was taken out of man."

And then the Scripture adds: "Therefore a man shall leave his father and mother and be joined to his wife, and they shall become one flesh" (verse 19). Hence, the man and the woman were *complete*. It is obvious therefore that God created marriage for His glory - so that, in His glory, you are complete and better together with your spouse than apart.

2. The Enemy of Marriage

However, when you *decide* to get married - whether you heard from God or not, whether you prayed about it or not - you must know that that there is an enemy waiting to rip that marriage to shreds. This is why you must not be ignorant of his devices, which can throw you off balance (2 Corinthians 2:11).

The devil's intention is to change your "we" to "I" and your "us" to "you". The devil's intention is to finish you through any outsider (physical or spiritual) that you allow to influence your daily thoughts and actions in marriage. I encourage you to read Genesis 3 and pay close attention to the process that led to the fall in the Garden. Remember that the word of God admonishes us to understand that the devil goes about like a roaring lion looking for whom to destroy (1 Peter 5:8).

The devil's primary mission on earth is to destroy anything good - whether it is a life, a marriage, a destiny, a pregnancy or a peaceful atmosphere; and he will use anyone or anything to achieve his scheme. So, the enemy of marriage is not your mother-in-law or the woman sent to lure your husband into sin; nor is it his best friends. The enemy is Satan "your adversary". Accordingly, when you decide to get married, be prepared for his attempts to break up your marriage. "Therefore take up the whole armor of God, that you may be able to withstand in the evil day (Ephesians 6:13).

Nugget 3
The most important thing in life is to have a real and thriving personal relationship with God.

This is KEY. When you have a thriving relationship with God, and the Holy Spirit in particular, you gain insight through wisdom and this helps you to defeat the enemy of marriage. You are able to stand when times get tough and you are strong, stable and in sync with the creator of marriage. Knowing and applying the word of God will help you navigate your way through the good and bad times and keep you from falling.

The Bible, in Genesis 3, says that the serpent was more cunning than any other beast that God had made. The serpent went to Eve, after carefully studying her, and asked "has God indeed said that you shall not eat of every tree of the garden?" What was Eve's response? She said, "We may eat the fruit of the trees of the garden; but of the fruit of the tree which is in the midst of the garden, God has said, 'You shall not eat it, nor shall you touch it, lest you die.'"

God knew that only a "you" can decide by yourself to disobey the instruction that He had given to a "we". In other words, when you operate as an individual in a marriage, you become weak and begin to do things that you should not do. You are prone to error when you singlehandedly make a decision that two people ought to make. Indeed, this is more likely to cause chaos, resentment, anger and arguments.

I am saying this for any married woman (or man) reading this book - you are no longer an individual because "two have now become one". So you must consider your spouse in everything that you do so that there will be no attack upon your marriage.

Nugget 4
Both couple in a marriage MUST have a thriving relationship with God. This helps the journey in the long run.

Eve could have waited for her husband before considering the serpent's suggestion. The devil is very cunning; he waits for the right opportunity to get into our minds and into our lives but we have to decide that we will no longer be his prey. The devil waited to get Eve alone; he attacked her by deceiving her. She was a new wife starting the real journey of life but he *finished* her. When he was done with her, he proceeded to finish her husband too.

Please repeat this confession every time you need it:

> *Satan you are a liar, you are under my feet. I will not fall for your tricks, so get away from me. My mind is alert and filled with the wisdom of God, so I rebuke the spirit of confusion now in Jesus' name! When I am ready to marry, you will have no place in my home or in our minds because you have already been defeated.*

3. Meaning of the Red Flags

As I have already hinted above, even though the words "complete" and "finished" are often used interchangeably, they mean different things, especially in the context of marriage. If one should marry the right man or woman, that person will be absolutely complete; but if one should marry a bruvva or a sista (I will explain these terms better in the next chapter), one is finished. I therefore decree and declare that you will marry the bone of your bone and the flesh of your flesh and you shall be complete, first in Christ, and then as a union under God.

Frankly, though, it rarely happens that people get finished in marriage without receiving prior warnings. In other words, there are usually telltale signs, better known as "red flags," that begin to appear, whether by natural or divine arrangement, to show that there will be disaster if a certain relationship ends in marriage. Sadly, however, most would-be couples tend to ignore these flags until it is too late.

Take Mina's case for example. From the moment she said "yes" to Steve, she began to experience a roller-coaster of strange events, and once the ring was put on her finger, things were just no longer the same. Conflicts arose - arguments, break ups/make ups, long hours of debating issues, disappointments, confusion, lack of trust and so much more.

Nugget 5
There are spiritual causes for restlessness and other problems that occur just before and after you are engaged.

I pray for you to get some insight the minute "strange things" begin to happen in your relationship. There is a reason, which you must not ignore.

Maybe you are about to propose or accept a proposal. You have someone in mind whom you love, and you believe you are ready. Darling, God says 'do not fear' but He wants you to take out more time to pray.

Are there some red flags you have been noticing in your relationship lately? Please list them below, and then take a break to say the prayer that follows.

Red Flags:
1.

2.
3.
4.
5.
6.
7.

Lord, I thank you for your amazing grace upon my life. As I am about to make a decision on who to who to spend the rest my life with – please, Lord, give me insight and barricade every road that leads nowhere! (Psalm 119:29 MSG)

Nugget 6
Hearing and heeding God's voice is your only guarantee against marital failure.

You must hear from God before you marry, beloved. You must hear His voice before you make or accept that marriage proposal. However, as I have noted before, personal relationship with God is indispensable for success in every area of life. You cannot hear God's voice clearly if you do not have a close relationship with Him. More importantly, a sound relationship with God is the foundation for all other successful relationships – your family, friends, spouse and children.

I speak from a place of love and experience today and plead with you to seek salvation and a close walk with God before you get into any relationship because, without God, a Christian marriage will not stand against the storms ahead.

If you are already married and you are faced with daunting challenges, believe me that a relationship with The One who ordained marriage is the key to deliverance from your troubles. Acknowledge Him, lean not on your own understanding but trust in Him and He will direct your path (Proverbs 3:5).

CHAPTER 2

WHAT IS BRUVVA?

The word *bruvva* (bruh-va) is the British pronunciation of *brother*. Have you ever heard British people speak? Their accent is fascinating and for a long time after I left London in 1995, I tried to continue speaking the same way I did as a teenager. I chuckle now as I remember how popular I was back in 1995 when I arrived in Nigeria for the first time in six years at a time when not many people had the opportunity to travel. Returning to Nigeria was a major culture shock but to ease the difficulty was the celebrity treatment I received in our little community because of my British accent.

Bruvva is a simple British slang for the male figure, whether a child or an adult. In this book, I chose to use it to describe a young man who is still rough around the edges. He could be selfish, immature, loud, mean, rude to women, maybe a narcissist or sexist, or an abuser; he is not a God-fearing man. This does not mean that British guys are bruvvas or that all men are "bruvvas."

A bruvva is what my father would have described as a "bubble gum boyfriend." A bubble gum boyfriend is just a boy; he does what he wants, when he wants. He has no mentor. He wants to hang out with his ex-girlfriends; in short, he is a womanizer. He is disrespectful of your time, effort and beliefs. He is easily angered; he may be violent, talks loosely, lacks wisdom and may not want to commit to you. These are just some of the characteristics you may have noticed but keep ignoring

However, I must alert you that there are certain issues that you just cannot ignore – else they will turn your marital life to a total wreck. These include anger, some spouts of jealousy, violence, disrespect, drunkenness, verbal and emotional abuse.

Listen, a bruvva is a guy. That's all he is - "some guy". He is not ready for marriage, though he may change later. At this time, this is not who you want to marry. If you marry a guy who is not quite ripe for marriage, you will end up with a man who is resentful and will neglect you because, as time passes, he will realize that he is not ready for all that comes with marriage: commitment, body changes due to pregnancy, nagging, someone always demanding to know your plans and movements, etc. - and eventually it may not work out.

Personal Experience

You may have suspected that Mina's story is actually my story. As I look back now, I realize that although my ex-husband and I were good people, we married at a time when we were not quite ready. We thought we were and we probably married each other for the wrong reasons too. Reasons such as:

I want to get married so I can leave my daddy's house. I want to marry because he proposed. I want to marry because he loves me. I want to marry because all my friends are married and my clock is ticking. I want to marry because he will help me stay in the country. I want to marry because I just have to be married by the age of 24.

Listen, you must know God's mind for you and if he is not it, then do not force it. If you guys cannot see eye to eye and both of you suck at compromise, communication and commitment, then you need to re-assess why you want to marry this person.

God's plan is to do exceedingly abundantly above all that we can ask or think, according to the power that works in us (Ephesians 3:20). However God needs us to be wise in making decisions about our future. That "bruvva" you feel stuck with is not exceedingly and abundantly; he is mediocre and less than God's promise for you. In other words, you know you can do better than him. So why must you marry that bruvva for real?

The Bible says in Amos 3:3 that "Do two walk together unless they have agreed to do so?" (NIV) - which simply means, can a relationship, partnership, marriage work if the two of you are not on the same page going in the same direction? Can it work if you are never in agreement?

There's a single young lady, reading this book right now and literally asking herself, "Why must I marry this bruvva?" Sadly, there is another married woman reading right now and asking herself "Why did I marry this bruvva?"

Listen, Christian sister, take all the time in the world now to assess your relationship:
- Is he born again?
- Am I born again?
- Does he know God?
- Do I know God, love God and fear God?
- Is he spiritually ready for marriage?
- Am I spiritually ready?
- Does this man even want children?
- What is his blood type? Is it compatible with mine?
- Does he believe in fasting?
- Has he read this book or other books about marriage?

Ask yourself the questions about values that are important for you. What about your deal breakers? This may be a good time to assess everything and write a list of your needs and hopefully he can sit with you to write his needs and then you both can compare to see if you can meet those needs.

Men have needs. What are his?
1.
2.
3.
4.

Women have needs. What are yours?
1.
2.
3.
4.

What cannot be compromised on?
1.
2.
3.
4.

Knowing the Basics

I just want you to know the basics and the most important thing to you. Does this man celebrate birthdays and holidays or was he raised not to celebrate Christmas? You have to know all of these things which seem trivial to you now until you get married and then begin to wonder why you did not put these them into consideration. In one of my live videos on social media, a lady asked me if it is possible to know everything before marriage, to which I replied "yes". You can know all things the same way you have your questions for an employer at the end of an interview. All the things that are important to you must be addressed before accepting the offer. If you are in school but fail to ask your employer if tuition reimbursement is offered before you take the job, you will be doing yourself a disservice because there are jobs that will reimburse your tuition.

So, go on and ask yourself: "Why must I marry this bruvva?"
Pause. Think. Open your eyes.
Are you done?

Are These Adequate Reasons for Marriage?

He is nice. I believe I am in love with him, and he with me. We've been together for years and years. We dated for one year, and I feel like we really connect. I am attracted to him. He has a good job, he is educated, he has met my parents, and everyone in my family loves him. He takes good care of me. He is a good guy.

It's funny to me now; I did not have all these answers yet I got married. Careless decisions lead to careless marriages.

Nugget 7
Do NOT marry a Bruvva! If you are set to marry one, cancel it. You are better off cancelling that wedding that failing in marriage.

You have time. Consider not the fancy things but consider this confession:

"If I keep my eyes on GOD, I won't trip over my own feet" (Psalm 25:15, MSG).

A few women may be lucky to meet a man who wants to marry them after a week of dating and they may end up happily ever after, but those are the exceptions. Most women do not have such luck. I wonder now what I was actually thinking at twenty six. I certainly was not thinking about the children, the effects of divorce, possibilities of adultery, physical or emotional abuse etc. This is why I am urging you now to take your time. Don't let anyone rush you.

Take your time to find out what exactly it is that makes you think "eternal" when you think of this person. If the both of you can come up with a decent list, you are off to a good start. Remember that women have a natural tendency to make decisions based on how we feel but men make decisions based on what they see. If you are a pretty woman that he sees value in, he will want you. However if you are 'feeling' some type of way about him, trust me, take note!

Stark Analogy

There is so much to consider when thinking of the rest of your life. Think of it as a prison sentence in a confined space with one person for the rest of your life. Is this person the type of person that you can be in a confined space with for the rest of your life?

I remember one winter weekend that it snowed so much and my ex and I were indoors for about three days. It felt like forever before it even started. I am certain that the energy he sensed caused him to convince me to go to my mother's house for the three days. We both knew that it would be a miserable three days so I excitedly packed and he happily drove me over to my mom's place. That's just crazy! This is one sign that a marriage is failing.

Choosing "the one" is not a decision that should be put upon you on the spur of the moment. From the time a man shows interest in you, before you even start to court, you should be praying to God to show you the deep and secret things about this person. If necessary, seek support from a man or woman of God and pray till you get an answer.

You and your suitor both need to seek godly counsel; but, most importantly, you need to be able to both pray together to ensure that you have the backing of God and the Holy Spirit to move forward. If you are having trouble doing this with him it is a *red flag*.

Somewhere in your heart perhaps you know something is not quite right – this is why it is imperative that you seek God and get confirmation. You need a word. *How do I get confirmation? How do I get a word? How do I hear from God?* The Bible is how you hear from God and He says in Psalms 32:8:

> *"I will instruct you and teach you in the way you should go; I will guide you with My eye."*

To hear from God:

1. You must be born again;
2. You must be baptized and be able to speak in tongues;
3. You must love God with all of your heart and all of your soul;
4. You must regularly study the Bible, pray and communicate with God.

This may seem a lot to do just to hear from God, but I tell you that going through divorce battles, restraining orders, property loss, child custody battles - and maybe hospitalization - is a lot to have to go through if you happen to miss it. I don't want you to miss it; so get the steps listed above done as soon as possible.

If you are having no issues in choosing 'the one' please keep reading because you may know someone who needs this information and you can be used by God as a vessel to change that person's life by helping them to learn how to hear from God.

The Curse Upon Eve

Marriage is no easy feat because of the curse placed upon Adam and Eve. Marriage was never intended to be a battle but it became a battle when the serpent tempted Eve and she in turn temped her husband. God came into the Garden that day, asking Adam what had happened; but Adam, being an immature man, did not cover his wife's nakedness. Instead, he threw her under the bus (like many men who lack wisdom do with their wives and the in-laws). We know that God knows all things; however God expects higher levels of wisdom from us when we are married or least He expects us to ask for it.

God blamed Adam because he was the head of the family; Adam threw Eve under the bus and then God cursed Eve saying "I will make your pains in childbearing very severe; with painful labor you will give birth to children. Your desire will be for your husband, and he will rule over you" (Genesis 3:16, NIV). The Message translation puts it best: "I'll multiply your pains in childbirth; you'll give birth to your babies in pain. You'll want to please your husband, but he'll lord it over you." Lord have mercy on married women because of what Eve did in the Garden!

Take Your Time

This is why you must take your time before choosing who you want to marry. If you rush in, chances are that you will rush out and I need us to stop doing this because divorce is now at an all-time high. Besides, many who rushed in have found themselves stuck with cruel men dishing out verbal, sexual and physical abuse and, sadly, many have lost their lives in this battle of marriage.

Anyone who wants to marry must remember that the curse that was placed on Eve and her descendants had been in existence before we came into the world. Thus, it takes God's full involvement to break it and give you a happy and successful marriage filled with love, support, romance, humility, prosperity, joy and all things good. This is how it was in the Garden before the fall of Adam and Eve, which broke God's heart.

What If You are on the Right Track?

Even if you think you are on the right track, with plans underway for your wedding day, it does not hurt to ensure that you BOTH have confirmation from God to proceed with the wedding. Remember that after all the money has been spent on the wedding, the marriage begins! If you are not at peace, please swallow your pride and postpone or cancel the wedding!

My wish for you is to have a successful marriage, bearing lots of good fruits and children. Marriage was created to glorify God; thus I pray for you that your marriage will glorify the Father in Jesus' name.

When you plan to marry, hopefully it is someone you have known for a long time or someone you can call your best friend. I know of a girl who met and married her man in less than two weeks. I don't have to tell you that she is now re-married. There are no time specifics but it should be someone that you know well enough; someone whose ways you value and whose presence never gets dull, tiresome or painful.

You want someone that your spirit is in total connection with. Someone who reminds you of how wonderful God is and how blessed you are. Someone who smiles at the sight of you and boasts in God about meeting you. Someone who understands you and respects you. Someone who is on the same page as you and you as him. Someone who shares your life-long dreams.

Even if you don't know what your lifelong dreams are at 24, it should be someone you don't have to struggle with. Someone who makes life easy for you. Someone who teaches you how to love. Someone who regards you in front of any and every one. Someone who, even when the doors are closed, still talks to you with respect, humility and love. Someone who loves God just because. It must be someone who knows that marrying you is his destiny.

You want someone who has talked to a man or woman of God about you and has asked you to come meet that man or woman of God. This shows that he is serious about you.

Some others meet their future partners, and they know in that very second that "this is it." For some, over the course of time, while attending the same church, school, fellowship, you find that you have things in common and you develop a friendship that later on blossoms into a relationship – it is not forced, it progresses over time. Finding someone like this takes patience. Once you are sold out to God and his righteousness, as well as His best for your education, career and family, all other things will automatically follow (Matthew 6:33).

What Do I Need to Know?

Whichever way you meet your "special person", the following are some of the assessments you must make:

1. His background: Where is he from? Who are his parents? How many siblings does he have? Is he the firstborn, only son, adopted child, troubled child? I have read a few books about the challenges of marrying a firstborn or two firstborns getting married; so maybe you should look into that also. The Yoruba people from Nigeria have a proverb that states that one must look at the home a man is from before determining what to call him. In simple terms, you can know a lot about a man by the part of town, state, country or family setting in which he was raised; or the schools, fellowships he is associated with.

2. Similarities: Are the two of you in agreement concerning your physical, emotional, spiritual and educational needs? What if you believe in furthering your education and he is not keen on this? Do you both enjoy cuddling, PDA (public displays of affection)? Do you want children? Does he want children? Do you both believe in God? Does he believe in tithes and offering? Do you go to church together? Do you celebrate holidays? Does he celebrate birthdays and holidays or is he the gloomy kind who can't be bothered?

For example, I am not always in the best moods during holidays, so I would not want someone who expects me to cook up ten dishes and make a fuss on Thanksgiving. I don't know if it's laziness or if it's the feeling of overwhelming compassion for those who are homeless during holidays, or if I just enjoy the lifestyle of the rich where everything is prepared by domestic helps or we go out to eat and just enjoy some quiet time indoors by the fire watching a movie. To quote Amos 3:3 again: "Do two walk together unless they have agreed to do so?" You have to find out if you two can take this walk of life together; so dig deeper, probe further.

3. Willingness to compromise: I met a man who always had to have his way on every single issue. He hated to lose; he hated to be told what to do; he hated to be advised; and he listened to no one. Is this the type of person you want to spend the rest of your life with? Check that. You may not always be in agreement about everything (especially social and political matters) but can you at least compromise? If not, you need to truly check that, remembering that whatever challenges you face now in your relationship, you will also face in your marriage.

4. Social skills: How does he relate to people? What are his social and communication skills like? Do you have to force him to speak to you? Are you able to converse for hours without arguments? Do you enjoy each other's company?

5. Goals/Dreams/Plans: What are his beliefs, dreams, aspirations and goals? Some people are so consumed by their goals and dreams that when they marry, they continue to single-handedly pursue those dreams – leaving out the one they married, failing to carry them along in their pursuit of happiness.

Whoever you plan to marry must be your prayer-partner and the one person who knows what your goals in life are. He must know what you are passionate about and vice versa. What are the two of you aspiring towards? What are your individual and corporate goals? Yes, you are now becoming a corporation – you are Adam and Eve working for the same boss; so you must know the assignment that you were both called for. You assignment is not just to marry and have children – it is bigger than that. As a Christian couple, you must know God's heart and plans for you. Right now, all you know is that He has "thoughts of good and not evil to bring you to an expected end," right? Nah, there was a purpose in bringing the two of you together.

This is pre-marital counseling 101. Ask yourself:
- What is the purpose of this union?
- Do you have a brother or a bruvva on your hands?
- Do you feel pressured to marry?
- What confirmation did you receive from God?
- Do you have peace concerning this man?
- Is there a scripture verse to back your decision (What scripture?)
- Any dream revelation? (Share the dream with your Pastor)

CHAPTER 3

A BROTHER – HIS ATTRIBUTES

I have taken time to explain the source and the specific usage of the term bruvva in the previous chapter. I did this mainly to be able to show you how a bruvva is different from a brother, whose attributes we are exploring in this chapter. And, no, I am not talking about your biological brother – as you will soon see. But, first, let's do a quick recap of who a bruvva is.

A bruvva is the guy you meet on your first date, who is trying so hard to impress you. He is dressed in his best shirt and clean jeans, wearing a pair of designer shoes (and not his sneakers), with a dash of his favorite cologne and smelling fresh. A bruvva is looking to date, have fun and get into your pants! If he has a good job, it is to spend the money on clothes; if he doesn't, he acts like he does and borrows his friend's car to take you out.

If he lives with his parents, he hides this fact; and if he doesn't, he wants you to know because he wants you to know that you can come over anytime. He will not want you to meet his folks because he's not sure where your relationship is headed. And if he brings you to his folks, don't be too happy about it yet; they probably know him for being a "ladies' man". So, when you say your "goodnights", listen well - they will probably ask, "So what's this one's name again?" That's your cue to exit the building and never return.

The "Brother"

A *brother* on the other hand is the man you meet for the first time, dressed nicely, polite and courteous. He shakes you by the hand and and doesn't hug you up to feel your boobs against his chest. He behaves like a gentleman, not trying too hard to impress.

He is a brother, in the sense that he is who he is, whether it's his sisters or his friends or it's you who are with him. He is a gentleman indeed. He takes you out and allows you to talk. He lets callers know that he is on a date with a beautiful lady (and he mentions your name). He doesn't keep you out too late because he understands that you have class or work in the morning. On a Saturday night, he gets you home early because you both have to be in church by 8 a.m.

A brother is a good bachelor. He is responsible. He can take care of the house. (This lets you know that you will share chores and when you are pregnant, you won't be left to scrub the floor or clean the bathroom, because he knows how to do it already). He can cook and take care of you when you happen to come over to meet his folks. And even if all he can cook is ramen noodles, at least you know that he is a man who doesn't see the kitchen as the woman's place.

A Christian brother with the fear of God may have offended you, but on Sunday morning, while listening to your pastor preach a sermon about forgiveness, the Holy Spirit convicts him and he immediately does the right thing to make up for the mistake. A bruvva might not have even heard that sermon because he got to church during the closing of the sermon, and he spent the rest of the service on the phone with his 'boys.' He might never have heard the sermon, even though you heard it, hoping that he heard it too. Even if you buy the CD and give it to him, he will simply toss it, promising to listen to it later. You will find it, six months later, in the same spot.

What Do Women Want?

Women want a man who knows when he is wrong, fixes it and refrains from doing it again, rather than a man who knows he is wrong, and covers it up with flowers. Worse still, women despise a man who doesn't have a clue that he has hurt their feelings, and walks around happy-go-lucky, while they are hurt and feeling sad. It ain't cute! It's only cute when a nine-month-old smacks you in the face, and smiles lovingly at you, while you are left holding your eye, hoping it won't fall out!

Brother man understands that you are from a large family; so he takes his time getting to know each of your siblings and brings you around his siblings. I told a man once that a man who has no regard for his mother will have no regard for his wife. It came to pass. So, watch his behavior - his tone of voice and his mannerisms with his mother, sisters, your friends, children, men of God, elderly people.

I don't expect you to search for Angel Michael but, ladies, there are men who ooze the Spirit of God and are genuinely good men with good intentions for you because of their relationship with God. If you find a man or woman like that, keep her. Go tell a man or woman of God what you have found and have them pray with you. It is crucial and the prayer will help you.

I pray that what you have found, the angels of God will keep for you till the day you say "I do." If you want a brother type of man, pray this prayer:

> *Oh Lord, send me a good man. I want to believe that there are good men out there, so help us to find each other now. Cause us to come in contact with each other and recognize Christ in each other when we meet. I will be careful to give you alone the praise, in Jesus' name!*

That 'bruvva' that makes you cry, that makes you

tell your friends what he has done now, that makes you angry when you see his call coming through, and that frustrates you is just a bruvva; move on!

In life, when you don't stand for something, you fall for anything. So if you know your worth, you will know how you should be treated. You will not let anyone walk all over you and cause you pain, hardship, strife and confusion. Listen, life is hard enough without adding relationship stress!

A Good Man Expresses Himself Well

A good man knows what he wants. He must be able to communicate well. I once met a man who could not finish his sentences. He would eat his words up and I always had a lost look on my face because I could never understand what he was trying to say. It doesn't mean he was not intelligent. On the contrary, he is very intelligent; he just didn't do too well in communicating with me. All these years later, however, he makes a conscious effort to get his point across clearly.

Women love to be appreciated because we go above and beyond for people we love. When I give and give but get nothing in return, it doesn't bother me as much as giving and not being acknowledged or appreciated for my giving. I know God is the rewarder of every man but, come on, your man must know when to say "Honey, you are doing a lot, and you have a lot on your plate, but you have been terrific this week!" It's very encouraging, and it makes you want to give more and more of yourself. No one should keep scores of their giving but rather be appreciative of one another. If your man is a taker, you better leave him alone.

Loving and caring go without saying. You will know if your man is loving and caring. Be sure though that his caring attitude is not expressed towards you alone, but also to everyone around him, and especially family members. We women want a man we are proud of and can show off; and when your man is loving and caring, all your girlfriends envy you, and wish that their men were like yours.

This sometimes has its own dangers, though. I have learned from other people's experiences that some wayward women tend to get attracted to such men. But you, as a praying woman, can deal with that effectively in your prayers.

Background Check

Even if first impressions make you feel like you're with a brother, you still must evaluate his family background and upbringing. Are his parents together? What's his opinion about monogamy and divorce? Did his father marry more than one wife? Are there cases of divorce in his family?

What is the foundation of this family you want to marry into? Look especially into his relationship with his female "household members." Is it cordial? Does he treat them with respect? Does he care for them? Are they close? Are they too close that you cannot fit in? Does he speak badly about his family?

Find out if he is a womanizer or a flirt, and test him to see if he is honest with you on the smallest things. Has he been married before? Did he lie about it? Are there any children you are not aware of? It wouldn't hurt to know who his ex-girlfriends are and what happened with them.

Some men were raised by single moms; so be sensitive. Some men were raised by abusive mothers; so get to know him very well and learn what triggers this good man. Nobody is perfect.

Lastly, how does he resolve conflict with you and others? Silently, violently, or prayerfully?

This is not excessive; you are choosing your life partner! What have you observed so far? Have you checked on your side too? Take notes. It will help.

Observations 1 – 10
1.
2.
3.
4.
5.
6.
7.
8.
9.
10.

Mina, Didn't You Know?

The first question a woman from a bad marriage is asked is "Didn't you know he was like that before you married him?" You must ensure you know what you are signing up for, so as not to get asked this terrible question!

Obviously, if your man is like most of us, he won't be perfect; however his good must outweigh his bad. You must both love, respect and honor each other dearly in order for things to work. Once again, please, do not ignore the red flags!

Nugget 9
The length of dating and the amount of drama involved do not constitute a reason why you should be tied. You are fit to be tied if you are compatible, respect each other, fear God and honor each another.

I often hear ladies say "We've been through a lot, so…" So what? You will go through much more when you marry him!

Ask yourself today, "why MUST I marry this dude?" And the answer better not be "because he loves me!" If you just told yourself that, close this book and hit yourself on the head with it.

Now, ask yourself, *what happens when he falls out of love with me?* What do you do then? May you not miss it in Jesus' name!

What To Expect

With my years of experience as a relationship counselor, I can tell you that some men do fall out of love with their wives. They get bored, they want variety, they want spice, they want to chase, and they like the hunt. Are you prepared to be different looking women just to spice up your marriage? Are you ready to keep your figure right, try different positions, remain active in the bedroom, gain little or no weight, keep your hair nice, speak appropriately at all times, love his family, serve hot meals, be submissive, be patient, be prayerful and be a mother to a grown man? This is what you must prepare for.

Watch the Temper

Watch out for curse words, angry tones, suppressed feelings, and generally the way he resolves conflict. But then, as I am asking you to do background checks on your man, I hope you are doing a background check on yourself too. Better still, I hope you know that he is doing a background check on you. Hey, maybe his sister gave him this book to read and as we speak, he is loving it and asking himself, "Why must I marry that sista?" (Laugh now but really though, what will your background check bring up, hmm?). No one is perfect; as scripture says,

ALL have sinned and fallen short of the glory of God (Romans 3:23).

Anger is a destroyer of any and every good thing. Indeed, anger has ended a lot of marriages faster than any other character flaw. Thus, you need to pay attention to the following questions so you can have a better understanding of what to expect if you marry the man in your life.

- Have you ever seen him on a bad day?
- Does he drink? Does he drink a lot?
- Have you seen the way he talks to people who owe him money?
- Have you ever seen him carry a baby in his arms or invite a baby to come sit on his lap?
- Have you ever seen him when he just found out he failed a test?
- Have you ever seen him sit and talk to his sisters, and or brothers?
- Have you seen the way he interacts with salespeople?
- Have you seen him when he hasn't gotten his way?
- Have you ever played a card game or sport with him?
- Have you talked about your future together?
- Have you planned how many kids you will have?
- Has he ever loaned you money? And when

you didn't pay him back, what did he do?
- Has he ever asked you for money?
- Has he held a job longer than a year? What is his view on abortion, teen pregnancy, rape, adultery, polygamy, cheating, war, sports, and the world today?
- Have you sat down to eat dinner more than three times a week?
- Do you have a lot in common?
- Do you have anything in common?
- Do you enjoy each other's company?
- Do you agree to disagree?
- Do you both compromise well?
- Do you both call each other equally to see how you are doing?
- Does he care enough to call to say goodnight?
- Does he pray at all?
- Does he take care of his mother, and siblings?
- Does he support your ideas?
- Does he call you when you get home (after a date with him) to make sure you got home safely?

Well, this book is not intended to make things hard for couples but to shed light on things you *may not* have thought about before. Watch the violent tendencies when he is mad and upset generally. I cannot stress enough that a man who physically abuses you did not just wake up one day and decided he was going to beat on you. Most likely, he had said so casually, or yelled it in anger but never did it, and he might have hit someone before.

Why don't you take all this time you have now to find about more about your man and his background? Hey, do a background check if you have to but do something other than just say "yes", with batting eyelids when he asks you to marry him.

Dealing With Doubts

Dear friend, as I earlier said, if you are worried, unsure, and asking yourself lots and lots of questions, just as I was, and you have any doubt in your mind, you must do something about it. We tend to call such negative feelings "butterflies" but you mustn't just downplay the situation. Find out God's plan for your life.

How? Fast. Pray. Talk to God about your situation. Contact your pastor/leader. Tell them your fears. Wait. Wait a little longer. Time will reveal many things if you can just patiently wait. While waiting, go back to school, learn something new, and pick up a hobby.

Perhaps, you and your boyfriend/fiancé have

been going through rough times lately, especially since news of the proposal, please note, as earlier mentioned, that this is not a mere coincidence. It is a red flag that requires you to pray fervently. You also need to chill out. Marriage is not by force!

Yes, we are not ignorant that the devil and his devices may be at work because the fool is against marriage and all that it represents. The devil is responsible for 99% of broken marriages because he creeps in on you when you are not praying.

Hopefully this book will prepare you for things yet to come. With that being said, I have to clarify my position. I love everything about love. I honor the sacrifice of marriage; it is a sacrifice for two people to come together and live a life of love and service to each another and it takes two very mature, self-less people to be able to do that.

When to Apply the Brakes

I do advise that if you and your partner are butting heads a lot for whatever reason, maybe you need to postpone any wedding plans for a season or two. So, if it is Winter right now and your wedding is set for the Summer of the following year (ample time to make up your mind), take the Spring season off to read this book again; fast, study the word of God, go for marriage counseling, seek a man/woman of God for counsel and pray hard about what you want to do.

By the grace of God, with fervent prayer, there will be a breakthrough for you and you will rejoice at the end of it all. I feel the troubled heart of a sister reading this book, going through some relationship problems. You are not alone. May God's will be done in your life.

One evening at a social club, the father of a young bride-to-be was giving out invitations to his daughter's wedding, taking place in a few weeks. His friend saw the name of the boy that would soon become the son-in-law and exclaimed, "Are you sure you want your daughter to marry this boy?!" When that father left the club, he was saddened by the question but a few days later, he shook it off and continued planning the wedding.

A year later, the same friend was called to mediate at the home of the couple who were about to split up. All efforts to save that marriage were in vain. He had been right to exclaim when he received that wedding invitation in the previous year. This is a perfect example of when a DIVINE direction was needed. It would only take a man or woman of God who HEARS God a few minutes to give good counseling and direction. Usually after good counseling, one should be at peace.

So, reader, I want you to be happy. But if your happiness is compromised by being rushed into something as huge as marriage, you should really take a step back, refresh your mind and ask yourself not "Do I love David?" but "Why must I marry David?" "Why must I accept his proposal?" "Of all the men, that I know, or have dated, why MUST I marry this bruvva?" "Why am I feeling that something is not quite right?" – It's because it is not!

If you can confidently answer the question on which this book is based and have sought counsel, then please go ahead and have a fantastic wedding and marriage. However, if you cannot answer the question, you need to pray again and again, asking God for direction. Talk to Him. Talk to your pastor or a pastor of your choice. Seek out a prophet of God (I cannot emphasize enough how much prophecy has saved me). God sends a man or woman of God to confirm what you already 'sense' in your spirit.

Learn to control the fears in your heart; communicate deeply with your inner spirit and follow your gut feeling because your instincts are hardly ever wrong.

A Good Man is a Pleasure to Watch

You will know a good man by the way he treats people. Does he have regard for people or does he think he knows it all and *'can't nobody tell him nothing'?* If you have a man that cannot be rebuked, advised, chastised, or corrected by his friends, family, pastor, counselor, or even lawyers, what you have is a problem: a big one! That bruvva has no regard for anyone nor does he have the fear of God, which scripture says is "the beginning of wisdom." You better watch out: that bruvva is not it. Shake your head and tell him 'you're not it.'

Sometimes, when you shake your head, they get it that "she's serious" and they sit up. But darling you don't want a man who sits up, you want a man who is *upright*. Yes!

CHAPTER 4

WISDOM IS THE KEY

The author of this book married a bruvva. There is no changing the truth about that. The shoe fits perfectly. He thought he was ready for marriage but he was not ready by a long shot. It was a big, lavish, society wedding that was preceded by months of bickering, breaking up, making up, confusion, control, harsh words, counseling, yelling, and so much pain.

Yet, they proceeded to get married because one would not let the other go and one was not bold enough to call it off and mean it. Red flags were at every corner of the streets this girl walked on. She would stop and stare at each red flag, use her human mind to rationalize and move past it. The bruvva would make excuses for bad behavior, they would break up, he would seek forgiveness, she would listen; soft at heart, she would take him back. It was a rollercoaster relationship.

How do you think the marriage fared? Just three months to their first wedding anniversary, they were separated. That's the fact.

Nugget 8

LOVE is not all you need. It can get you in trouble if it is not supported with the right ingredients. The love of God is the ULTIMATE!

Anatomy of Love

For you to be able to truly love someone, you must love yourself and you MUST love God with all of your heart, your body and your soul. If you love yourself, you must want the best for yourself. You must have a high regard for yourself. The Lord that made you was not asleep when He created you, so why must you settle for someone who makes you feel inferior?

Love is a word that you cannot comprehend in the flesh; you can only comprehend it through the Word of the living God. Try to read 1 Corinthians 13. It speaks of what Love is. I have met men - brothers, in-laws, cousins, and friends - who are 1 Corinthians 13 and their women cherish them for it.

When you find a good man or woman, you will know and you will protect that asset jealously. If you don't protect it jealously and you allow it to slip out of your hands or you take advantage of this rare thing, you end up regretting it. Most times, it's the relationships in which the assets are great that the devil attacks first. You should watch out if you have a good man or woman. Let your prayer continually be, *"Lord, I thank you for this good and perfect gift that you have given me. I know that when the enemy comes in like a flood, you Oh God will raise a standard against him, in Jesus' name I pray!*

Dear friend, let me categorically say this, you cannot love another human being if you don't love yourself and love God. You cannot understand love except you know God; except you are His son or daughter and believe in Him wholeheartedly. You do not have the capacity to love unless you first love God. Any marriage without God's love is not founded on love.

You must understand this partner of yours in-depth. We love God simply because He first loved us. He gave His only son to die for us. He is all-sufficient. He is a provider, He is a comforter, and He is the all-in-all, the all-knowing being, the sovereign God.

To truly love God, you must KNOW Him. In the times when you are down, when the devil brings trouble your way, your love for God, which breeds trust and confidence in Him, will let you say to yourself, "I know that God will make a way. He won't leave me nor forsake me."

Once again, you must know this bruvva of yours. Delete the "tall, dark and handsome" fantasy from your "list" and sincerely ask yourself if this dude is all or most of the following:
- A listener, friend, friendly, born again and church attending brother.
- A support system, trustworthy, hardworking, generous, educated, presentable, expressive, appreciative, loving, caring, ambitious, financially dependent.

You *may* also add 'attractive' to the package. Then and only then should you evaluate if this dude meets the criteria and qualifies for the great role as your husband and forever lover!

If you don't look into the above areas, you will realize there is a mismatch when you are attending a church function and he goes off to a game; or you attend the naming ceremony of a friend and he tells you to go without him; or your best friend is getting married and he doesn't understand why you must pay all that money to be in the bridal party.

Your ideal man should be one who truly loves, appreciates and acknowledges you. Imagine being at your friend's party, and you have been there setting up with them, laying table covers and hanging up the balloons along with other friends. Just then you spot your partner walk into the room. Your face lights up and you go to meet him as he walks in, but he goes around greeting people and does not acknowledge you till he is done or not at all. What happens to that smile of yours? What happens to that expectation of a hug or a kiss?

Little disappointments create big disasters.

Catalyst of Favor

The Bible says he who finds a wife finds a good thing, and obtains favor from the Lord (Proverbs 18:22). Does one ignore a good thing? No. So, tell yourself, "I refuse to be ignored. I am a good woman."

You are fearfully and wonderfully made. He who finds you has found a good thing. He will obtain favor. If he treats you shabbily, give him the red card straight up and accelerate your car. Just move on, dear sister, because where God is taking you, there is no room for setback or apologies after the fact. You need someone who will be by your side because he knows that he has a good woman.

Take Pride in Me

When I was sixteen, back at home in Lagos, Nigeria, I remember that my first love - a young man who is still my good friend till this day - would come over to our house and ask me to walk with him down the street. Being the lazy teenager that I was, I would refuse him. But one day, he pleaded that I walk down the street with him so that the other young men in the neighborhood could know that *the pretty girl from Jand (London)* was his girlfriend.

Apparently, a few of them had told him he was lying and could not possibly be dating me at the time. So I walked with him one day as he asked and as we walked down this busy road in our community, I will never forget the look on his face and the confidence with which he walked. That day, I got home and my perception of men changed. They want to be with someone they are proud to show off!

Snare of Pre-Marital Sex

You need someone in your life who makes you feel like you are the only one for him and he needs to feel the same about you. If you are 24, you don't need a man who tells you these things because he wants you to sleep with him and stain that perfect picture of you on your wedding day. You need a man who understands that you are *worth the wait*. I don't care how hard it is for you or him; you both need to understand the concept of waiting till marriage. The Bible says if the foundation is destroyed, what can the righteous do? (Psalm 16:3).

First of all, at sixteen, I was too young to be in a serious relationship but I am thankful for the Redeemed Christian Church of God, Acme Parish, Lagos, because that minister of God in the Teens Church probably saved me from pre-marital sex. I remember one service in our Teenager's class, our Pastor had asked us all to stand up if we had a boyfriend. She made it sound so fun, so hip, so interesting that a lot of young girls stood up. How naïve we were! She then said, "Go home today and tell him, 'I can't be your girlfriend anymore'".

Then she explained that a young boy of 16 to18 had only one thing in mind: sex. She explained that there were children being born and thrown in the dumpster. She narrated how a sexually transmitted disease killed a young girl in the church. I was terrified. I got home that afternoon, opened my window and looked over into Ben's father's house and asked him to stand at the window. He did. And there, I told him, "I can't be your girlfriend anymore. I do not want to die." I slammed the window shut and ran to my room.

Interestingly, almost 16 years later, he sent me a text asking why ladies were so fake and pretentious unlike women from back in the day. I couldn't help but laugh. I sent him a reply, saying, "Next year, you will marry and you will find the right one." Ben is now married and he has a beautiful daughter.

Sex before marriage is a way of destroying your foundation. Don't do it. It doesn't last long; it's a temporary feeling. It clouds your brain and if that was his sole intention, very soon you won't hear from him anymore because he will be on to the next one.

There is so much that happens after pre-marital sex. It feels almost like when Eve and Adam had been tempted and their *eyes were opened*. It opens up a can of worms that a young girl cannot deal with, especially when you give it up to an immature man who does not understand how much you cherished your virginity from a young age. Now, every time some argument arises, you get in your feelings because you know you gave up something you should not have given up and the person who took it has the audacity to stomp all over your heart while cheating, lying and putting other people above you. You become extremely sensitive.

Trust me, you do not want to be in this position. Keep it locked until you get that rock. Do not have sex just because you are engaged.

A 35-year old lady sent me a message the other day and when I asked her if she had been sleeping with the man she was dating, she said "Yes, because I know that we will end up getting married." Sister, if you cannot control your body, you cannot control your mouth. If he cannot control his body, how do you trust that he will control his hands from hitting you one day?

Christian marriages are no longer Christian because we are not sincerely following Bible principles. We simply select the laws we want to obey and do what we want to do, how we want to do it. When trouble comes knocking, we begin to read the book of Psalms, forgetting that we are the ones digging holes. We date married men, we fornicate, we drink, we party all night, we skip church, we don't pay our tithes, we fight and argue a lot, we cannot control our tempers; yet we claim that we are Christians!

CHAPTER 5
MARRIAGE IS A GIFT

I will not apologize for saying that if you are a Christian, your first mistake will be to marry a man who doesn't love God or who has not made peace with God. You are making a mistake if you are with a man who doesn't believe in God, who claims he is an atheist, or who is just plain old indifferent.

The Bible says that "The fool has said in his heart, "There is no God" (Psalm 14:1). And if he is not a fool, is he a born again Christian who attends a Bible-believing church? Oh, did

I hear you say, "Hmm, my man is a good guy. He doesn't drink, doesn't smoke. He is educated, and he doesn't have to be churchy or born again. He is a good man."

Okay, I agree that there are many great men out there who do not go to church; but if he is a Christian, why is he not going to church?

Be Equally Yoked

Very importantly, the Bible clearly warns:

> *"Do not be unequally yoked together with unbelievers. For what fellowship has righteousness with lawlessness? And what communion has light with darkness? And what accord has Christ with Belial? Or what part has a believer with an unbeliever?" (2 Corinthians 6:14-15).*

So, you have it there - there is no room for marrying an unbeliever in the Kingdom. However, if you have married an unbeliever or someone of another faith – perhaps in your time of ignorance – you have to pray and trust in God to have his way in the life of your spouse.

Also, I have no issues with interracial marriages. I believe they make the world a beautiful place, provided both individuals understand and appreciate each other's culture. Love conquers fear, and the love of God conquers all things. With love, faith, and hope in God, all things are possible.

Stand Firm

The only way your marriage can stand the test of time is for it to be built on the foundation of God's word. Enter into a marriage with God's intention of being together FOREVER.

There are too many marriages broken, too many hearts hurt, too many children missing the love of a parent, too many court cases, too much physical, emotional, and verbal abuse, too much malice, too much hatred in the world. All these lead inevitably to divorce if found within a marriage. If resolution is possible, a prophet of God will reveal God's mind to you. If not, God Himself will make a way.

Seek godly counsel. Ask for prayer. Find yourself a prayer partner or join my prayerline.

Divorce Triggers

In your marriage, avoid the following pitfalls that have led to the collapse of many marriages:

D – Discussing your partner/marriage with others is not a great idea.

I – In-laws and others giving you negative advice creates bad energy.

V – Verbal abuse, emotional or physical abuse will end a marriage.

O – Outsourcing for love, sex and or affection from friends and exes.

R – Remembering past arguments and showing disrespect.

C – Communication gap, cheating, lack of common sense is a problem.

E – Expecting more than what you give in your marriage is ridiculous.

If you are currently married, I pray that God richly bless your marriage. Ecclesiastes 4:9-12 says, "Two are better than one, because they have a good reward for their labor…" I bless God for all those in good marriages; though there are good days and bad days, God will continue to fuel your marriage with love and unity in Jesus' name.

Someone is reading this book; you are the one always giving, and working to keep your marriage because your partner is carefree. The Lord says He will touch your partner if you stay in the place of prayer and obey Him. Things will change for the better if you do not let it escalate to violence by your actions or reactions. Keep praying and keep believing for change. He will make a way for you, even where there seems to be no way.

Intricacies of Marriage

The union of two is a very intricate, delicate one. You must realize that you are two people, from two different parents, upbringings, backgrounds, values, and family systems, coming together to live under the same roof for the first time. For some, it's like two teenage sisters sharing a room – they will fight a lot. For others, it's like best friends sharing a room on campus; it will be a great lifetime story because they remain friends forever.

Marriage will come very easy for some; yet some others just have to work extra hard to get along and accept the newly found negative traits they will begin to observe in their spouses, alongside the positive ones. A wise friend of mine once said that when your spouse irritates you and you are not getting along, just take one of their good qualities and do what women do best (besides shopping) - blow it out of proportion!

Magnify this one good quality so much that it blinds you from focusing on the fact that he leaves the bathroom door open after doing a Number 2. Simply get up and shut the door, remembering (from all the magnifying) that he gives you a back rub every other night when you come home stressed from work!

Be a Good Man

Women are great magnifiers. We can elaborate and tell a story in such a grand way. So when a man buys us something or treats us real nice, we magnify it and make it bigger than it really is and we make the man feel good because he has done something great. Sorry but this does not apply to men who think they can "buy" a woman.

So if you are brother, and not a bruvva, do things or continue to do things that will make your woman magnify your efforts. And the Lord will crown those good efforts in Jesus' name.

All Will Be Well

I am fully aware that no marriage is perfect and that everyone who is interested in keeping their marriage spends time and effort doing their best to keep all parts functioning well. It takes divine grace, real love, patience and long-suffering in order to have a happy marriage.

There's a lady reading this book and you are a victim of physical abuse. Don't cry. Wipe your tears. You are the apple of God's eyes. He will restore your lost glory and you will smile again. He says concerning you, I will do a new thing, behold it shall spring forth. Weeping endures for a night, but joy comes in the morning (Isaiah 43:19; Psalm 30:5). Get up and keep your head up darling. God loves you, it is well with you and your children. Read Joel 2:25. It encourages me daily.

CHAPTER 6
PUT THAT "BOOK" BACK

Mina is now the single mother of two lovely children. She works hard to sustain herself and the children; she trains them up in the way they should go so that "when they are old, they will not depart from it" (Proverbs 22:6). She shoulders the burden of two people but she has confidence that her God is preparing a table.

She seemed to have been prepared for her present status though. While she was married, she was alone. Her bruvva was frugal, stayed out late a lot, consumed alcohol every day, led a secret life, spoke and treated her harshly, behaved irrationally, skipped church often, wouldn't listen to correction, couldn't take care of his child, and above all, he cleaved unto his family more than his wife.

She on the other hand lacked wisdom too. She complained about him a lot, treated him the way the devil wanted her to see him and often spoke with anger to the man she was supposed to respect. These behaviors are a recipe for disaster and divorce. Such a marriage will not work.

Perhaps, you are in a similar situation as Mina. Maybe not with two children, but one, three, four or more. You are carrying the loads of two people. God will settle you this year. If you are a child of God, and you love Him - He will settle you.

Get right with God now, plug yourself into a Bible-believing church, join a department in church, serve God with all of your heart, and join my prayerline if you find it hard to pray by yourself. Serve God. Find a mentor in your leaders at church. Seek out an anointed marriage coach like me to pray with you and give you wise counsel.

Mina, that 24-year old girl, had a very hardworking and ambitious man with a lot going for him; but he was just not a *brother*. She should have put that book back. Over the years, though, she has learned that life is too short to live it miserably. So, reader, get going now and become all that God has called you to be. No more hindrances. Find a way out of the mess. Make up your mind that this is your year!

Nugget 10
Never judge a book by its cover and never compare your situation with someone else's, thinking that they are better off. You just don't know what they are facing in the privacy of their own home.

Confess Positively
Are you a Christian lady in courtship already? Open your eyes, heart, ears, and let God direct you both. I want you to cultivate the habit of fasting and praying together now. Confess out of your mouth the things that you want. It will become a habit and, soon, you will start to see the manifestation of the things you have spoken. If you call your man trouble, he's going to give you trouble. If you perceive something is wrong, it probably is wrong. If your spirit cautions you,

it's because there's something up somewhere. For every fear, there's a reason, and if it is the devil, tell him he is under your feet. But I beg you; dot your "i"' and cross your "t" and God will help you.

Luke 1:37 states that "For with God, *nothing* shall be impossible" (KJV). It's a favorite verse of mine. So say what you want, believe it and you will surely get it.

Here is the confession of a single lady:

> *Father, I thank you because I am living in my best seven years. I believe in your word that it is not good for a man to be alone; so I thank you Father because you are now sending me a good man after your own heart who will love, cherish and adore me. I pray that you prepare me now as a helper comparable to him so that I will honor, respect and comfort him always. I call this done now in Jesus' name. Amen.*

Traits of a Brother

As a summary of my earlier description of a brother, I have garnered some important details from some Christian women I spoke with about things to look for, to determine if a man is marriage material. As a woman, I know that no man is perfect and he will not come in a total package but we want a man that LOVES God first and then if he has the following traits, we will be even happier.

1. God-fearing
2. Spirit-filled
3. Kingdom-focused (Pays tithes, offerings, seeds)
4. Good upbringing
5. Financially stable
6. Emotionally stable and mature
7. Healthy
8. Truthful, faithful and loyal
9. Caring and supportive
10. Hardworking
11. Humble
12. FUN!

If you have a partner and he or she is not all you have spoken to God about and more, you better put that "book" back up on the shelf. Seek to meet a man that has the traits listed above or at least 85%.

Your Own Character

With all that has been said, have you looked

inward at your own character? What are your own faults that you need to work on and pray about? What are those habits that you need to drop? How do you resolve conflict? Are you a gem or a great deal of trouble? Check yourself too, my dear. No one is perfect, but God says, "walk before me, and be thou perfect" (Genesis 17:1, KJV). It's a daily walk, darling.

A woman who has anger issues, low self-esteem, low sex-drive or who lacks respect, argues a lot, keeps malice, proves stubborn, wise in her own eyes, cooks badly, lazy, boring, etc., is not ready for marriage.

Embrace Your Season

This is your season; so if you are single, enjoy being single. If you are in love, enjoy being in love. If you are divorced, take time to heal, discover yourself and enjoy finding love again. If you are a single mom, embrace your season of motherhood; determine to be the best parent that your children could ever need and remember that whenever you are ready, a good BROTHER is out there.

My pastor wrote a book called *Table for One* which helps single women in what may seem like a lonely walk; so I encourage you to get that book as well. It will bless your life as it has blessed mine.

Nugget 11
Men want honor, respect, peace and good sex; women want love, attention, security and joy. Do your best to seek after the heart of the one you love.

David sought after God's heart and loved him so much that God continually forgave him, as long as he was penitent. Let's learn this one character trait of *seeking after the heart of the one we love* and when two people do this consistently, there will be no need for divorce.

I am trusting God with you that when I meet you, it will be to share testimonies of God's greatness. I hope that you have been blessed by my book. If you have, please send me an email. Pray without ceasing and God will answer. Prayer is the absolute key!

I wish you the very best in life and love. I pray the Holy Spirit himself directs you and I sincerely hope you make the right decision!

CHAPTER 7
THIS TIME

I was finishing off Chapter 6 when the words, "this time", caused me to think for a few minutes. It occurred to me that God still has something to say to those who have the opportunity of "this time."

There are some women reading this book right now; they are single mothers - separated, divorced, widowed, and some have never been married. They have one thing in common: the lack of a brother. These words are labels used to describe you, just as the woman with the issue of blood was described in the Bible (Luke 8:43–48). She had no name. She was labeled.

A *label* can be a form of *limitation*. We will not be limited in Jesus' name. So, perhaps, you were involved with a *bruvva* – who is now nowhere to be found in your life - and you are left with the baggage of hurt and pain, coupled with a child or children to take care of. Perhaps you were married before to a brother but things happened; perhaps he misbehaved and you gave him the red card.

Perhaps you had a child or two by a *bruvva* and years later you are still not married to him. Perhaps you are a woman who lost her husband and now you are by your lonesome self (except for God and your children). Perhaps you are married but alone in your marriage like that 24-year-old lady was. Perhaps your child or children's father is not much to write home about and the two of you butt heads all the time.

Perhaps you have never been married and you are longing for companionship and a life of happiness like some women that you know. Perhaps some of these women are your friends, sisters, mothers, teachers, lawyers, counselors, pastors, cousins, nieces, aunts, grandmothers, mothers-in-law or just acquaintances. Take heart; there's hope for you too.

Be On Your Guard

All of the different categories of single women that I mentioned above are still prone to being involved with a bruvva again and again. These women are sometimes the most vulnerable because they are alone and in need of a friend, lover and confidant. These women are prey for *bruvvas*.

I will be honest with you. Some men will come after you just because they know you are separated, divorced, widowed or single - past the age of marriage. Some men will want to take advantage of your vulnerability. Some men will find you an easy target. **Change their mind quickly.**

On the flip side, there are many men out there who want to wipe those tears, love you, cherish you and share your burdens. They are out there; they may not be as many as the predators, but they are out there.

I have a firm belief that there is someone out

there for you and for me and we shall meet one day. Delay is not denial. Keep making positive confessions. That brother is closer than you think.

This chapter is dedicated to any woman who falls in the categories listed. This chapter was created just for you at the last minute because God, your Father in heaven, finds you special and worth the addition of another chapter.

God says: *"When I created you, I did not sleep or slumber. You are created for a purpose. You have a destiny to fulfill and an assignment to carry out."*

Some of us have made mistakes in the past but God is saying: *"If you draw close to me, I will draw close to you."*

Are you ready to draw closer to God and obey the words written in Matthew 6:33?

Sister, no matter what you have been through, your mess is your message; your test is your testimony. No matter how many men have used and abused you, no matter how many times your heart has been broken, no matter how hurt or lonely you are, God is still in the business of making a way where there seems to be no way. He is the ALMIGHTY God. The God who told me He would give me double for my trouble. That God is your God.

Joel 2:25 says that "I [God] will RESTORE unto you ALL the years that have been lost…" Get your Bible and receive that word today. Confess it. Repeat it. Digest it. Meditate on it daily.

Be very aware of the *bruvvas*. Go back to the items on your contents page. If he doesn't meet the wonderful criteria, PUT THE BOOK BACK on the shelf before he messes you up.

This time, you must be wise. This time, you must be strong. This time, you must be bold. This time, you must be firm. This time, you have to be confident in who you are as a child of the Most High God and you MUST be spiritually sensitive. This time, you must be VERY prayerful.

And, as an added bonus, you should talk to God when you find yourself attracted to a man or he is attracted to you:

Lord, is there any road here? If there is please open

my eyes to see and give me the peace in my heart that I need. Show me the deep and secret things that my natural eyes cannot see and barricade every road that leads nowhere. (Psalm 119:29, MSG)

When you ask God about a relationship, He answers you because God's plans for you are good, not evil.
You have a destiny to fulfill. Do not be sad. Do not be depressed. Do not give up hope. Do not put yourself down. Have no regrets.

Rather, do what that 24-year-old did. She found God at all costs.

Please find a Bible-believing church and PLUG yourself in. There is a REWARD for those who seek God diligently. Connect with a man or woman of God whom you can talk freely with and discuss your burdens. He or she will not only pray with you but they will war with you and guide you. That's what you need right now.

Be faithful to God and He will surprise you. I cannot stress enough that prayer is the KEY. When you have no strength to pray, join my prayer-line. When you are not happy, attend a church service in your area and be LIFTED and feel free to talk to your mentor.

The joy of the Lord is my strength and yours as well.

If you are not born again, I would like you to know that you cannot enjoy the joy of the Lord if you do not know the Lord. If you wish to know the joy of the Lord, please say after me:

> *"Lord Jesus, I am a sinner. I confess that Jesus Christ is Lord. I want to know the joy of the Lord; therefore, Lord, come into my life and take over today, in Jesus' name I pray." (Amen.)*

What you need to do now is ask God to help you to connect with a Church that will impact your life and help you experience a turnaround.

Confession:

Father, I thank you because I am now born again and my name is in the Book of Life. I believe that you have raised somebody for me who has used her experience, your super-power and her abilities to help to me.I thank you, Father, for the amazing exploits of her life and ministry. I declare that, henceforth, I shall walk in your perfect will for my life. I confess that I am living in the best season of my life and I will be careful to bring glory to your name in all that I do! In Jesus' mighty name. Amen!

ABOUT THE AUTHOR

Seyi Hopewell is an author, inspirational speaker, and a women empowerment leader. She is a graduate of The University of Maryland, from where she obtained her Master's degree in Human Resources Management and Business Management.

Seyi holds seminars across the country for both men and women who want a better marriage and she especially cares for those who have been through bad marriages.

She is the founder of Sheba Women Ministries, where she inspires #MomsWhoPray and her followers all over the world to join her in prayers at 5am CST. Her purpose in life is to serve God and save lives.

Seyi continues to inspire lives across the world through The Seyi Hopewell Show and through her speaking engagements.

NOTE

NOTE

NOTE

NOTE

NOTE

NOTE

www.ingramcontent.com/pod-product-compliance
Lightning Source LLC
Chambersburg PA
CBHW070649050426
42451CB00008B/323